ANGRY BIRDS™

COMICS

WHEN PIGS FLY

COVER ARTWORK BY: PACO RODRIQUEZ
COVER COLORS BY: NICOLE PASQUETTO

ORIGINAL SERIES EDITS BY: DAVID HEDGECOCK
COLLECTION EDITS BY: JUSTIN EISINGER & ALONZO SIMON
COLLECTION PRODUCTION BY: CHRIS MOWRY

Laura Nevanlinna, Publishing Director
Jukka Heiskanen, Editor-in-Chief, Comics
Juha Mäkinen, Editor, Comics
Jan Schulte-Tigges, Art Director, Comics
Henri Sarimo, Graphic Designer
Nathan Cosby, Freelance Editor

For international rights,
please contact licensing@idwpublishing.com

Thanks to Jukka Heiskanen, Juha Mäkinen, and the Rovio team for their hard work and invaluable assistance.

ISBN: 978-1-63140-592-1

18 17 16 15   1 2 3 4

IDW

Ted Adams, CEO & Publisher
Greg Goldstein, President & COO
Robbie Robbins, EVP/Sr. Graphic Artist
Chris Ryall, Chief Creative Officer/Editor-in-Chief
Matthew Ruzicka, CPA, Chief Financial Officer
Alan Payne, VP of Sales
Dirk Wood, VP of Marketing
Lorelei Bunjes, VP of Digital Services
Jeff Webber, VP of Licensing, Digital and Subsidiary Rights

www.IDWPUBLISHING.com

Facebook: facebook.com/idwpublishing
Twitter: @idwpublishing
YouTube: youtube.com/idwpublishing
Tumblr: tumblr.idwpublishing.com
Instagram: instagram.com/idwpublishing

ANGRY BIRDS
BEST NEST TEST

AB 2014-066

PIGGY ISLAND, WHERE THE ANGRY BIRDS ARE HOLDING AN IMPORTANT MEETING!

SO... WHO CAN TELL ME WHAT THIS IS?

UMM, IS THIS A TRICK QUESTION?

IT'S A NEST, RIGHT? GO AHEAD AND SAY IT!

YOU SAY IT! I'M NOT GONNA SAY IT! IT'S OBVIOUSLY A TRICK QUESTION!

WRONG!

IT'S A NEST, RIGHT?

I KNEW IT.

1

WRITTEN BY: **PAUL TOBIN** • ART AND COLORS BY: **THOMAS CABELLIC**

2

I THINK WE'VE DONE IT!

THERE! DOESN'T THIS FEEL BETTER?

AND WE'RE HIGH ENOUGH UP TO KEEP A LOOK OUT FOR THE PIGS!

SO THIS NEST IS *MUCH* BETTER THAN THAT OLD...

PLIP

IS IT STARTING TO RAIN?

PLIP

PLOP

ONE HOUR LATER...

SO... I'VE DECIDED AGAINST ROCKS, BUT...

I'VE BEEN HARVESTING RUBBER FROM THIS RUBBER TREE, AND LET ME PRESENT...

...OUR NEW HIGH-TECH RUBBER NEST!

HMMM. IS IT COMFORTABLE?

IT SURE IS!

LET ME SHOW~!

JUMP!

THWOOOP!

!

FLOOOP!

GAHH!

7

THREE HOURS LATER...

WATER?

OKAY. I HAVE A TO-TALLY NEW IDEA. WE CAN MAKE A NEST OUT OF WATER.

SURE! SEE? THE EGGS FLOAT!

TRUE.

GAHHH!

BUT... YOU DON'T.

THUMP!

SPLOSSHH!

ACKKK!

BLUB BLUB

9

THE END!

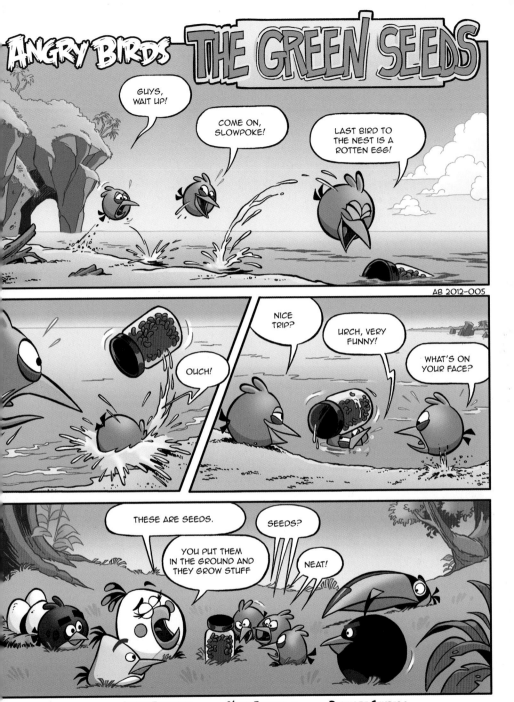

AB 2012-005

WRITTEN BY: **JANNE TORISEVA** • ART BY: **CÉSAR FERIOLI** • COLORS BY: **DIGIKORE STUDIOS**

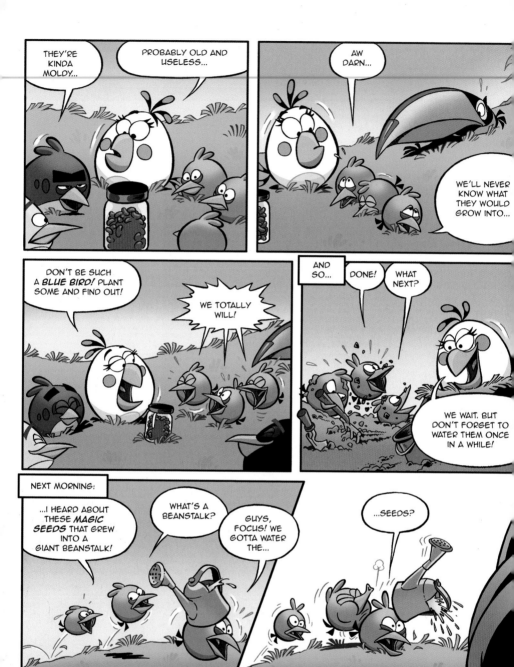

(SNORT) MMMM, WHAT'S ON THE MENU TODAY, CHEF?

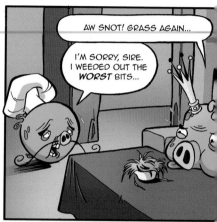

AW SNOT! GRASS AGAIN...

I'M SORRY, SIRE. I WEEDED OUT THE *WORST* BITS...

YOUR ROYAL PIGNESS! YOU HAVE TO HEAR THIS!

THE BIRDS ARE ALL IN A FLAP OVER SOME GREEN EGGS!

YOU ARE DISTURBING THE KING'S GRASS DINNER!

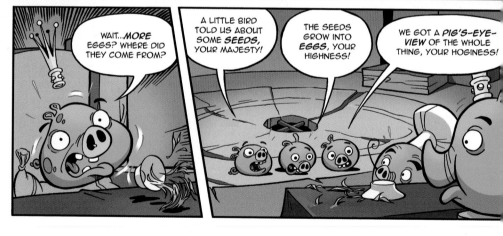

WAIT...*MORE* EGGS? WHERE DID THEY COME FROM?

A LITTLE BIRD TOLD US ABOUT SOME *SEEDS*, YOUR MAJESTY!

THE SEEDS GROW INTO *EGGS*, YOUR HIGHNESS!

WE GOT A *PIG'S-EYE-VIEW* OF THE WHOLE THING, YOUR HOGINESS!

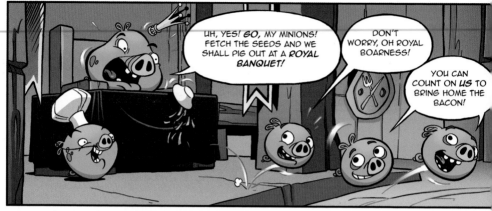

WHAT ABOUT THE PIGS? THEY *STOLE* FROM US! WE CAN'T LET THEM GET AWAY WITH THIS!

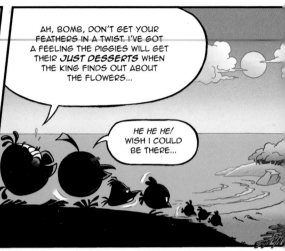

AH, BOMB, DON'T GET YOUR FEATHERS IN A TWIST. I'VE GOT A FEELING THE PIGGIES WILL GET THEIR *JUST DESSERTS* WHEN THE KING FINDS OUT ABOUT THE FLOWERS...

HE HE HE! WISH I COULD BE THERE...

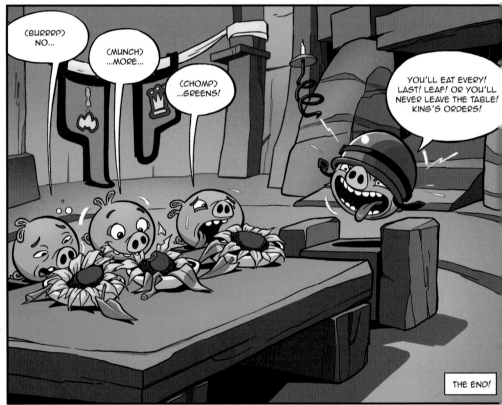

(BURRRP) NO...

(MUNCH) ...MORE...

(CHOMP) ...GREENS!

YOU'LL EAT EVERY! LAST! LEAF! OR YOU'LL NEVER LEAVE THE TABLE! KING'S ORDERS!

THE END!

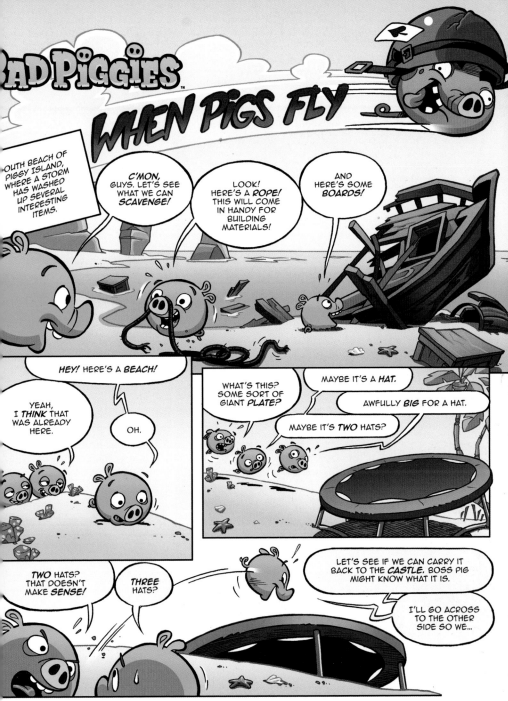

BAD PIGGIES
WHEN PIGS FLY

"SOUTH BEACH OF PIGGY ISLAND, WHERE A STORM HAS WASHED UP SEVERAL INTERESTING ITEMS.

C'MON, GUYS. LET'S SEE WHAT WE CAN *SCAVENGE!*

LOOK! HERE'S A *ROPE!* THIS WILL COME IN HANDY FOR BUILDING MATERIALS!

AND HERE'S SOME *BOARDS!*

HEY! HERE'S A BEACH!

YEAH, I *THINK* THAT WAS ALREADY HERE.

OH.

WHAT'S THIS? SOME SORT OF GIANT *PLATE?*

MAYBE IT'S A *HAT.*

AWFULLY *BIG* FOR A HAT.

MAYBE IT'S *TWO HATS?*

TWO HATS? THAT DOESN'T MAKE *SENSE!*

THREE HATS?

LET'S SEE IF WE CAN CARRY IT BACK TO THE *CASTLE.* BOSS PIG MIGHT KNOW WHAT IT IS.

I'LL GO ACROSS TO THE OTHER SIDE SO WE...

WRITTEN BY: PAUL TOBIN • ART BY: CÉSAR FERIOLI • COLORS BY: DIGIKORE STUDIOS • LETTERS BY: PISARA OY

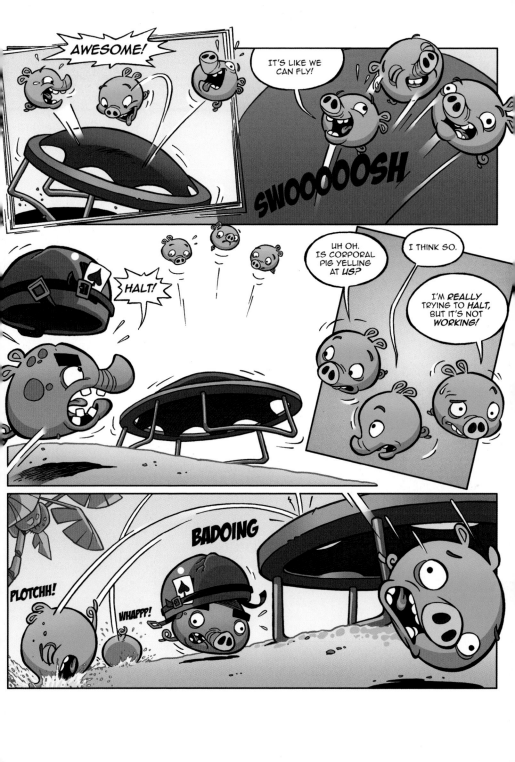

ANGRY BIRDS

HUUUUUUUUUNG-RYYYYYYYYYYY...

WHERE'S CHEF PIG?

HE'S... IN A BALLOON, SIRE.

THAT MAKES SENSE. HOPE HE'S LOOKING FOR EGGS.

MWAH HA HA! I'M LOOKING FOR EGGS!

....AND NOW I'VE FOUND THEM!

WRITTEN BY: **FRANÇOIS CORTEGGIANI** • ART BY: **GIORGIO CAVAZZANO** • COLORS BY: **DIGIKORE STUDIOS** • LETTERS BY: **PISARA OY**

IN THREE! TWO!

LET'S GET SOME!

NO "GETTING SOME" FOR A BIT, SINCE CHEF PIG'S MOVED OUT OF RANGE...

AW MAN!

GET OUTTA HERE, PIGGY!

TIME TO THROW MY WEIGHT AROUND!

HRM?

BWAH HA HA HA!!!

MISSED AGAIN!

ANCHORS AWAY, TAKE *TWO!*

OH ME, OH MY!

BOMB, HELP! HE'S GOING FOR THE EGGS!

?

TOO LATE! HAHAHA... THE EGGS ARE *MINE!*

HEY WAIT, I HAD SLACK. WHAT'S GOING ON?

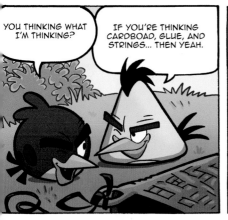

YOU THINKING WHAT I'M THINKING?

IF YOU'RE THINKING CARDBOARD, GLUE, AND STRINGS... THEN YEAH.

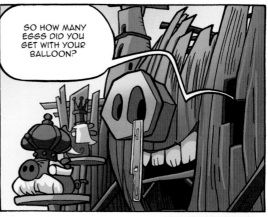

SO HOW MANY EGGS DID YOU GET WITH YOUR BALLOON?

UH... BALLOON? WHAT BALLOON? I'VE BEEN OUT PICKING MUSHROOMS FOR YOU ALL DAY!

YUCK... MUSHROOMS AGAIN...

HE'S HERE, YOUR MAJESTY!

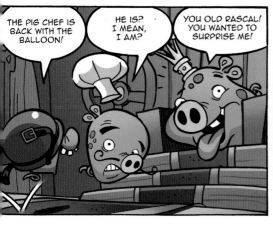

THE PIG CHEF IS BACK WITH THE BALLOON!

HE IS? I MEAN, I AM?

YOU OLD RASCAL! YOU WANTED TO SURPRISE ME!

YEAHHHHHHH... SURPRISE...

BAD PIGGIES
SURPRISE

ON SOUTH BEACH, WHERE MANY INTERESTING THINGS WASH UP!

WHAT'S THAT?

SOME SORT OF GLASS CONTAINER

!?

YEAH. IT'S FULL OF EGGS.

HEY. WAIT A SECOND...

EGGS!

EGGS!

RUN! RUN! RUN!

KING! KING! KING!

EGGS! EGGS! EGGS!

WRITTEN BY: **PAUL TOBIN** • ART BY: **AUDREY BUSSI & ISA PYTHON** • COLORS BY: **DIGIKORE STUDIOS** • LETTERS BY: **ROVIO COMICS**

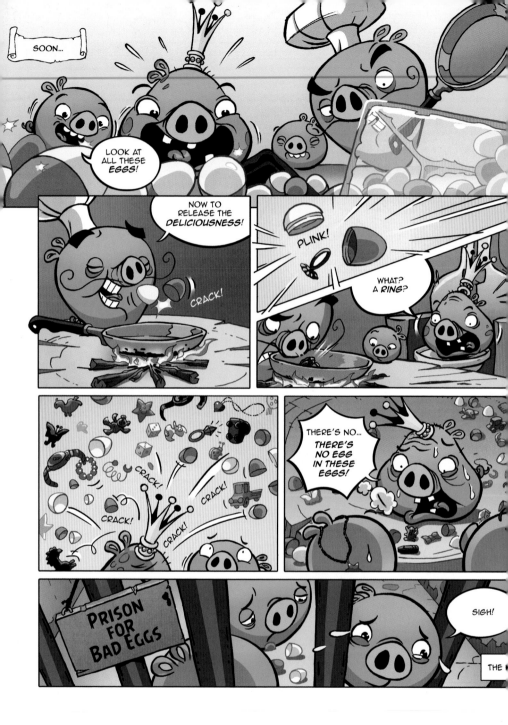

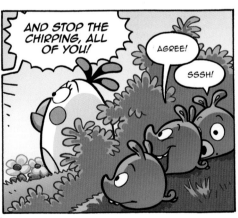

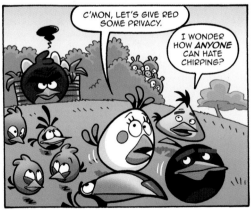

WRITTEN BY: **JANNE TORISEVA** • ART BY: **GIORGIO CAVAZZANO** • COLORS BY: **DIGIKORE STUDIOS** • LETTERS BY: **ROVIO COMICS**

AHEM.

HOW MANY YEARS MUST A BIRD WATCH EGGS...

BEFORE YOU CAN CALL IT A BIRD...!

SQUEEK!

THAT UNBEARABLE NOISE...

THE HORROR...

NOISE? HORROR? WHAT ARE THEY SQUEAKING ABOUT?

HARD TO SAY, YOUR MAJESTY. THAT'S ALL WE'VE GOT OFF THOSE MORONS.

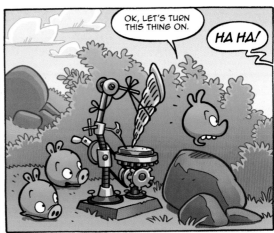

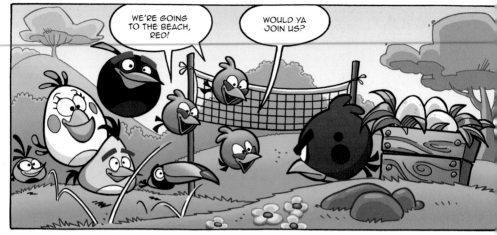

WE'RE GOING TO THE BEACH, RED!

WOULD YA JOIN US?

SOMEONE HAS TO GUARD THE EGGS, YOU KNOW.

WELL, *I* COULD GUARD THE EGGS FOR A CHANGE.

UH... THANKS, BUT I'M NOT IN A MOOD FOR THE BEACH TODAY.

SIGH. AS YOU SAY, RED.

C'MON, LET'S *GO!*

THE ANSWER, MY BIRD, IS CHIRPIN' IN THE WIND...!

EEEK!

EEEK!

HELP!

WHAT... BLUE BIRDS! BUT THEY WENT TO *ANOTHER* DIRECTION!

HELLP!! EEEK!

WHAT'S WRONG, BOYS? GET UP FROM THERE!

EEEK!

EEEK!

I SHOULDN'T LEAVE THE EGGS FOR A SECOND... BUT I CAN'T LEAVE THE BLUES IN TROUBLE!

HELP!

EEEK!

OKAY, BOYS. WHAT'S THE...

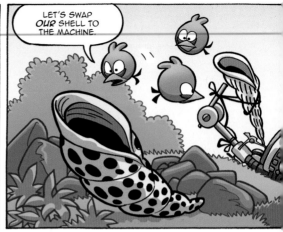

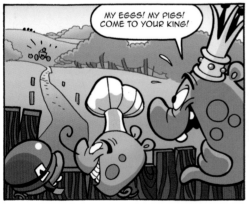

WRITTEN BY: **JANNE TORISEVA** • ART BY: **PACO RODRIQUES** • COLORS BY: **JOSEP DE HARO**

I'M GOING TO GET RID OF THE EGGS. I MEAN...

WE KNOW WHAT YOU MEAN.

...OF...

...THE EGGS?

GET RID...

THEY WANNA GET RID OF THE EGGS?!

THAT'S WHAT THEY SAID, YOUR PIGGNESS.

THIS MAKES NO SENSE...

ELEMENTARY! BIRDS ARE BORED OF WATCHING THE EGGS AND WANT TO GET RID OF THEM NOW! MAKES *PERFECT* SCIENCE SENSE!

SCIENCE?

PREPARE MY CHAIR, WE'LL GO TO NEGOTIATE WITH THE BIRDS IMMEDIATELY!

YES, YOUR MAJESTY!

WRITTEN BY: **ANASTASIA HEINZL** • ART BY: **MARCO GERVASIO** • COLORS BY: **DIGIKORE STUDIOS**

OH RED, I'M SUCH A FOOL! I'M SO SOOORRY!

CALM DOWN, CHUCK. IT COULD HAVE BEEN WORSE. BUT WE HAVE TO REACT, QUICK!

MATILDA! THE BLUES! YOU WILL GO TO THE BEACH AND TRY TO FIND SOMETHING WHICH COULD REPLACE THE RUBBER BAND.

CHUCK! BOMB! YOU'LL STAY WITH ME TO GUARD THE NEST...

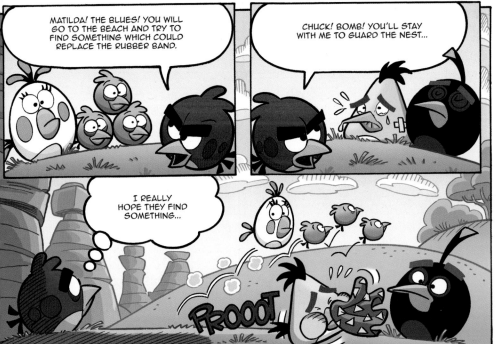

I REALLY HOPE THEY FIND SOMETHING...

PROOOT

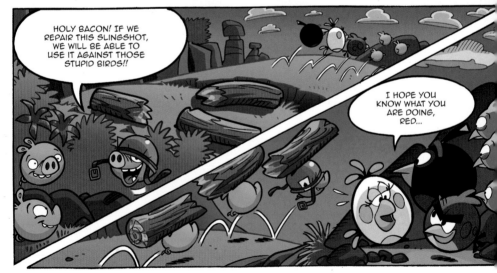

NIGHT FELL ON PIG CITY...

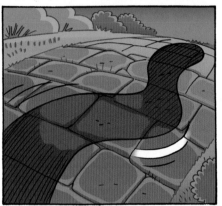

OUCH! WATCH OUT!

SSSSSHHH!! WE'RE NEARLY THERE!

SSSSSS!!!

AAAAAH!!! A SNAKE!

LET'S BE BRAVE, GUYS.

AAAAAAAAAH!!

Artwork by Paco Rodriques
Colors by Digikore Studios